Bible Studies

PERPLEXING SCRIPTURES

CONVERGE
Bible Studies

PERPLEXING SCRIPTURES

JOSH TINLEY

Abingdon Press

Nashville

PERPLEXING SCRIPTURES
CONVERGE BIBLE STUDIES

By Josh Tinley

Library of Congress Cataloging-in-Publication Data has been requested.

ISBN: 978-1-4267-8953-3

Series Editor: Shane Raynor

14 15 16 17 18 19 20 21 22 23—10 9 8 7 6 5 4 3 2 1

Manufactured in the United States of America

CONTENTS

CONTENTS

ABOUT THE SERIES

Converge is a series of topical Bible studies based on the Common English Bible translation. Each title in the *Converge* series consists of four studies based around a common topic or theme. *Converge* brings together a unique group of writers from different backgrounds, traditions, and age groups.

HOW TO USE THESE STUDIES

Converge Bible studies can be used by small groups, classes, or individuals. Each study uses a simple format. For the convenience of the reader, the primary Scripture passages are included. In Insight and Ideas, the author of the study guide explores each Scripture passage, going deeper into the text and helping readers understand how the Scripture connects with the theme of the study. Questions are designed to encourage both personal reflection and group conversation. Some questions may not have simple answers. That's part of what makes studying the Bible so exciting.

Although Bible passages are included with each session, study participants may find it useful to have personal Bibles on hand for referencing other Scriptures. Converge studies are designed for use with the Common English Bible; but they work well with any modern, reliable translation.

ONLINE EXTRAS

Converge studies are available in both print and digital formats. Each title in the series has additional components that are available online, including companion articles, blog posts, extra questions, sermon ideas, and podcasts.

To access the companion materials, visit

http://www.MinistryMatters.com/Converge

Thanks for using Converge!

INTRODUCTION

The pastor of a church I once attended had strong feelings about children's Bibles. She believed that children could and should learn stories and teachings from Scripture in an age-appropriate manner, but she was wary of putting a Bible into a child's hands.

There's no lack of gratuitous violence in Scripture. And there's plenty of sexual content. If you go by the Motion Picture Association of America's film ratings system or the Entertainment Software Rating Board standards for rating videogames, you'd have to conclude that no child should ever open a Bible without parental supervision. Many churches give their children Bibles when those children begin the third grade. Do third graders really need to read about Jael's gruesome, tent-peg-to-the-temple killing of the Canaanite general Sisera (Judges 4:18-22)? Do they need to peruse the comprehensive list of unlawful sexual relations in Leviticus 18? Probably not without guidance from an adult.

Children grow up in the church singing "Jesus Loves Me" and getting to know a God who is patient and forgiving and eager to have a relationship with every person in all of creation. What happens when young people encounter Scriptures where God appears to lack patience and grace? What happens when they read about God commanding King Saul to kill every single living being among the Amalekites— men, women, children, and animals (1 Samuel 15:1-3)? What happens when they discover that God executed a couple for being dishonest about their offering money (Acts 5:1-11)?

Pick up your Bible. For Christians, this anthology of 66 books, letters, and other writings (73 if you're Roman Catholic and 76 if you belong to one of several Eastern Orthodox churches) is our canon. For as long as this collection of writings has been in place, Christians have been in near universal agreement that our Bible is authoritative and inspired by God. Christians have different understandings and interpretations of what "authoritative" and "inspired by God" mean, but we all recognize the Bible as our holy book.

The word canon comes from the Greek and means "rule" or "ruler." For religious communities, a canon defines the community's relationship with the divine and establishes guidelines for how people within the community should live. Christian communities, with a few exceptions, consider our canon closed. There is no process for adding or removing books from our Bibles. Even so, Christian communities end up creating their own canons, whether intentionally or unintentionally. There are certain texts that come up frequently in worship or in the youth room or in the children's Sunday school wing. And there are certain texts that we never read in worship nor bring into the Sunday school class or youth Bible study.

But the obscure and unsavory Scriptures that we don't like to deal with are still Scripture. Those who are new to the faith or those who are critical of Christianity can easily find Luke 14:26, where Jesus says, "Whoever comes to me and doesn't hate father and mother, spouse and children, and brothers and sisters—yes, even one's own life—cannot be my disciple." And even if we intend for our youth Bible study on Elijah's showdown with the prophets of Baal to conclude with 1 Kings 18:39, there's nothing to stop a teenager from reading on to verse 40, where Elijah rounds up his defeated rivals and kills them. We may not like to deal with these verses, but they're in our canon; and we have to answer for them.

Judaism has a different understanding of canon than Christianity does. The Jewish Bible, or Tanakh, contains the same writings as the Protestant Old Testament, albeit in a different configuration. But the Tanakh is only one piece of the Jewish canon. Judaism holds that divine revelation has been passed down both in written form, the Tanakh, and by oral transmission. The oral tradition was recorded in written form in the Mishnah around A.D. 200. The Jewish canon also incorporates the teachings and writings of learned sages, called rabbis, who have analyzed, interpreted, and debated the Tanakh and Mishnah. Jewish scholar Jacob Neusner explains, "[Judaism] does not find its definition in a book—e.g. The Old Testament. Its generative principle is quite the opposite: God did not resort solely to a book to convey and preserve the divine message. It was through teachings, which could be transmitted in more than a single form."[1]

In Judaism the wisdom and authority of a text goes beyond the text itself. Discussions of and extrapolations from the text are also considered sources of revelation. Christians do not have this luxury. But perhaps we can learn something from our Jewish brothers and sisters and their approach to divine revelation and the authority of Scripture. These difficult texts should be the starting points for conversations about God and who we are as God's people.

The purpose of this study is to facilitate those conversations. It will examine Scriptures in which God appears petty and capricious, Scriptures in which God and/or God's people are responsible for mass killing, and Scriptures in which Jesus says things that seem to contradict whom we know Jesus to be. This study will raise more questions than it answers; and the answers to some of these questions may never be clear. But I hope that as you go through this study, you will find the courage to address Scriptures that you'd rather ignore and will begin to see how God's love and grace is at work even in the most troubling texts.

---

1 From *Introduction to Rabbinic Literature,* by Jacob Neusner, (Doubleday, 1994); page 6.

1

OVERREACTION?

GOD AND THE EIGHTH COMMANDMENT

SCRIPTURE
2 SAMUEL 6:1-11

[1]Once again David assembled the select warriors of Israel, thirty thousand strong. [2]David and all the troops who were with him set out for Baalah, which is Kiriath-jearim of Judah, to bring God's chest up from there—the chest that is called by the name of the LORD of heavenly forces, who sits enthroned on the winged creatures. [3]They loaded God's chest on a new cart and carried it from Abinadab's house, which was on the hill. Uzzah and Ahio, Abinadab's sons, were driving the new cart. [4]Uzzah was beside God's chest while Ahio was walking in front of it. [5]Meanwhile, David and the entire house of Israel celebrated in the LORD's presence with all their strength, with songs, zithers, harps, tambourines, rattles, and cymbals.

[6]When they approached Nacon's threshing floor, Uzzah reached out to God's chest and grabbed it because the oxen had

stumbled. [7]The LORD became angry at Uzzah, and God struck him there because of his mistake, and he died there next to God's chest. [8]Then David got angry because the LORD's anger lashed out against Uzzah, and so that place is called Perez-uzzah today. [9]David was frightened by the LORD that day. "How will I ever bring the LORD's chest to me?" he asked. [10]So David didn't take the chest away with him to David's City. Instead, he had it put in the house of Obed-edom, who was from Gath. [11]The LORD's chest stayed with Obed-edom's household in Gath for three months, and the LORD blessed Obed-edom's household and all that he had.

INSIGHT AND IDEAS

I saw *Raiders of the Lost Ark* in the theater in the summer of 1981. I was four, almost five. While I consider *Raiders* one of the greatest pieces of art ever projected on a giant screen, and while it runs 115 minutes (five minutes short of two hours, and 37 minutes shorter than *The Dark Knight*), I had a hard time making it through the entire movie. I snoozed through significant chunks of it. A couple years later, my family got cable television; and we caught *Raiders* on one of the movie channels. Again, I had trouble staying awake for the entire 115 minutes.

So I didn't really appreciate the cinematic masterpiece that is *Raiders of the Lost Ark* until I was older. But two scenes stuck with me from those early viewings:

- The opening scene in which swashbuckling archaeologist Indiana Jones retrieves a golden idol from a Peruvian temple, only to trigger a booby trap and narrowly avoid being crushed by a giant boulder. (Everyone remembers that scene.)

- The scene toward the end when the Nazis who have confiscated the ark of the covenant from Dr. Jones take the ark to an island in the Aegean Sea and decide to open it, wanting to test their prize before taking it back to Hitler in Germany. (*Raiders* is set in the 1930s, so the Nazis are the principle antagonists.) Opening the ark proves to be a mistake.

If you've seen the movie, you know what happens when the Nazis (led by French archaeologist-for-hire René Belloq) remove the lid from the ark. They find that the shattered remains of the tablets that once bore the Law given to Moses have been reduced to sand. Then they find something else: death. Light fixtures surrounding the ark explode; the Nazi soldiers' guns go off; and a storm (with lightning and everything) erupts within the ark. Spirits, possibly seraphim, descend on those gathered, eliciting awe and then terror. A flame emerges from the ark and the fire of God strikes dead all of the soldiers who were foolish enough to watch as the ark was opened.

Then the major players—Belloq and the Nazi leadership, including Major Arnold Toht—get theirs. The divine fire melts them like a nine-year-old boy with a fire fetish melts his plastic action figures. Indiana Jones and his partner and love interest, Marion Ravenwood, survive by shutting their eyes and turning away from the ark.

The moral of the story: The ark of the covenant is not to be trifled with.

THE ARK: DANGEROUS NOT ONLY FOR NAZIS

George Lucas and Steven Spielberg (the producer and director, respectively, of the Indiana Jones films) didn't come up with the idea that the ark is deadly for those who don't respect it. We find it in the Old Testament, 2 Samuel 6:1-10.

The ark makes its first appearance in Exodus 25 when Moses meets with God atop Mount Sinai, or Horeb. (Mount Sinai and Mount Horeb are two names for the same mountain.)

While God dictated to Moses the Law and the terms of the covenant between God and Israel, God gave Moses instructions for building an ark—a box made of acacia wood—to hold the tablets on which the Law is written. God told Moses the dimensions of the ark, how to decorate the ark (where to place the depictions of winged heavenly creatures), and how to transport the ark. The transportation instructions were simple: "Make acacia-wood poles and cover them with gold. Then put the poles into the rings on the chest's sides and use them to carry the chest. The poles should stay in the chest's rings. They shouldn't be taken out of them" (Exodus 25:13-15).

The Israelites carried this sacred box through the wilderness of Sinai for 40 years and into their new home in Canaan. The ark went before them during their conquests under Joshua and when they settled the land between the Jordan River and Mediterranean Sea. We don't read about the ark in the Book of Judges, but we know that it spent some time in Gilgal before finding its way to the city of Shiloh during the time of the prophet Samuel. The neighboring Philistines captured the ark for a time but couldn't hold it, and it wound up in Kiriath-jearim. It stayed there until the reign of King David, who decided to bring the ark to his new capital, Jerusalem.

The story of King David's finally bringing the ark of the covenant (the one that would melt so many Nazi faces) into Jerusalem comes up frequently in youth ministry curriculum. David was so overcome with joy that he danced "with all his strength before the LORD" (2 Samuel 6:14), accompanied by "shouts and trumpet blasts" (verse 15). David's wife Michal (daughter of his predecessor and rival, King Saul) watched her husband dance "in a linen priestly vest" (verse 14) and lost "all respect for him" (verse 16). But David was not ashamed.

This story is great for youth because 1) it shows dance as a form of worship, and the idea of praising God through dance is a welcome one for young people who have trouble staying awake during more staid expressions of worship; and 2) David dances before God boldly and without embarrassment.

The events that precede the ark's triumphant arrival in Jerusalem and David's celebration don't come up nearly as often. When David assumed the throne as Israel's second king,

17

the ark resided in Kiriath-jearim. It ended up there because the people in its previous home, Beth-shemesh, couldn't handle it. God killed seventy Beth-shemites as punishment for looking into the ark (1 Samuel 6:19-20). (Unfortunately for them, they hadn't seen *Raiders of the Lost Ark*.)

David decided that the ark belonged in Jerusalem. Getting it there proved troublesome. David assembled a group of thirty thousand "select warriors" to accompany the sacred box on its journey. But he and his men made the unfortunate decision to transport the box on a "cart" (2 Samuel 6:3). (To be fair, the text says that it was a "new cart.") Carts are great for getting television and DVD player sets from one end of the church building to the other. Carts are less effective when it comes to moving acacia-wood boxes across rocky terrain.

The group David had assembled started from Abinadab's house, which was on a hill. Abinadab's sons Uzzah and Ahio rolled the cart down the hill. Ahio walked in front of the cart; Uzzah walked beside it. The other thirty thousand people who were there "celebrated in the LORD's presence with all their strength, with songs, zithers, harps, tambourines, rattles, and cymbals" (2 Samuel 6:5).

Everything was going well until the oxen pulling the cart stumbled. Uzzah, knowing that he would have a disaster on his hands should the ark tumble from the cart, "reached out to God's chest and grabbed it" (2 Samuel 6:6). God was angry that Uzzah had touched the ark and struck him dead.

Uzzah was just trying to help out. He had good intentions, but he broke a rule and paid with his life. The ark remained in the house of Obed-edom in the city of Gath for three months before David tried again to bring it to Jerusalem.

CRUEL AND UNUSUAL

The eighth amendment of the United States Constitution, right there in the Bill of Rights, says: "Excessive bail shall not be required, nor excessive fines imposed, nor cruel and unusual punishments inflicted."

It's not terribly specific. "Excessive" and "cruel and unusual" mean different things to different legislators and judges. But the point of this amendment is simple: The punishment should be proportional to the crime.

This concern for proportionality didn't originate with the founders of the United States of America. In fact, it is nearly identical to an item in the English Bill of Rights of 1689. But the principle of a punishment fitting the crime goes back much farther.

The Law in Leviticus 24:19-20 says, "If someone injures a fellow citizen, they will suffer the same injury they inflicted: broken bone for broken bone, an eye for an eye, a tooth for a tooth. The same injury the person inflicted on the other will be inflicted on them." This "eye for an eye" precept is commonly known as *lex talionis,* a Latin phrase meaning "law of retaliation."

Lex talionis seems harsh to twenty-first-century ears. The international community tends to look down on nations that have branches of law enforcement devoted to gouging eyes, pulling teeth, and breaking bones. Such an approach to criminal justice offends our human rights sensibilities. But this ancient law was actually written with human rights in mind. If someone chops off your hand, the most you can do in retaliation is to chop off one of that person's hands. You are not allowed to respond to a maiming by killing your attacker's family and burning down his village.

So even Leviticus, a book that many Christians regard as the chief source of obscure maxims that don't apply in the twenty-first century, warns us not to go overboard with punishments.

The idea of proportional punishment is written into God's law. Yet when it comes to punishing poor Uzzah, God doesn't seem to adhere to the same standard. And unlike the antagonists in *Raiders of the Lost Ark*, Uzzah wasn't a Nazi. He wasn't planning on harnessing the ark's power with an eye toward world domination. He was just trying to keep the ark from falling off the cart.

In his book *God Behaving Badly*, Old Testament scholar David T. Lamb argues that God's punishment of Uzzah was warranted. He points out that God had given the Israelites clear instructions on how to carry the ark, and the Israelites neglected to follow those instructions.

Of course, most of us have failed to follow instructions, even divine instructions, and have not been stricken dead as a result. But, Lamb adds, the ark was so sacred and so powerful that adhering to instructions for its care and handling was absolutely necessary. "Handling the ark was inherently dangerous," he writes, "like handling radioactive materials. If people do not use proper precaution when transporting plutonium, people die."[1] Indeed, the stakes for transporting the ark were even higher. (It's worth noting that, in 1 Samuel 6, when the Philistines agree to return the ark to Israel, the Israelite priests instruct the Philistines to send the ark on a cart drawn by two calves. It is unclear whether these instructions come from God or are invented by the priests themselves.)

Lamb also says that he believes that the audience was a factor in God's punishment of Uzzah. The crowd of thirty thousand chosen to travel with the ark was both large and influential. For this reason, according to Lamb, God had to be clear about expectations and the consequences of not following procedures and could not allow the mishandling of the ark to go unpunished. "With an audience of the entire nation," Lamb writes, "[God] did not want to send the message that obedience is optional."[2] He notes that the Israelites' disobedience had to be punished in a way that would get their attention.

Perhaps Uzzah's infraction wasn't as minor as we might think. But there are plenty of other instances in Scripture where God inflicts a seemingly excessive punishment. Prior to the destruction of Sodom and Gomorrah, in Genesis 19, God's messengers told Lot and his family to flee the city,

---

[1] From *God Behaving Badly*, by David T. Lamb (IVP Books, 2011); page 28.
[2] From *God Behaving Badly*; page 29.

saying, "Don't look back." But Lot's wife couldn't resist. On her way out of town, she looked back and "turned into a pillar of salt" (Genesis 19:26).

'ACCEPT COMMUNISM OR DIE'

Lest we dismiss such as excessive punishment as the work of a pre-Jesus, Old Testament God, we should consider the story of Ananias and Sapphira in Acts 5:1-11.

Acts tells us that the first Christians held everything in common. Those who joined the young Christian movement turned over all of their income and assets to the apostles, who would redistribute it as needed. Barnabas, for example, "owned a field, sold it, brought the money, and placed it in the care and under the authority of the apostles" (Acts 4:37). Barnabas did what was expected.

A couple named Ananias and Sapphira did not. Ananias, with his wife Sapphira's knowledge, sold a piece of property and kept "some of the proceeds" for himself. He gave the rest to the apostles. Peter, a leader among the apostles, knew immediately what Ananias had done and launched into a litany of questions: "Ananias, how is it that Satan has influenced you to lie to the Holy Spirit by withholding some of the proceeds from the sale of your land? Wasn't that property yours to keep? After you sold it, wasn't the money yours to do with whatever you wanted? What made you think of such a thing? You haven't lied to other people but to God!" (Acts 5:3-4). Ananias didn't even get a chance to make his defense. He dropped dead on the spot.

A few hours later, Sapphira, not knowing what had happened to her husband, met with Peter. He asked her about the sale of the property, and she confirmed the false amount that Ananias had reported as the selling price. Peter responds, "How could you scheme with each other to challenge the Lord's Spirit? Look! The feet of those who buried your husband are at the door. They will carry you out too" (5:9). And with that, Sapphira dropped dead too.

The Brick Testament website—which recreates biblical events and illustrates biblical teachings using Lego bricks and offers a super-literal and often irreverent take on Scripture—entitled its treatment of the Ananias and Sapphira story "Accept Communism or Die." I appreciate the humor. But the text suggests that Ananias and Sapphira were punished not because they refused to play along with the apostles' system of income redistribution but because they were dishonest about their commitment to the church. Peter told Ananias that he had lied about how he would use the money and accused Sapphira of scheming to cheat the Holy Spirit.

Lying before God is a grave offense. But should it be a capital offense? How many of us have been guilty of not fulfilling our pledge to the church? I will confess that I have been. And God never smote me for it. Still, when I read the account of Ananias and Sapphira's death in Acts 5:1-11, it reinforces for me the importance of being faithful to commitments—both commitments to God and commitments to the community of faith.

Perhaps the lesson we take from these perplexing Scriptures is not that God is ready to strike us down for seemingly minor infractions but that these infractions are not as minor as they seem. Even if we think that God went overboard in punishing poor Uzzah, Uzzah's story teaches us that God's instructions should not be taken lightly and that there are consequences for failing to follow these instructions, even if those consequences don't involve being zapped or turned into sodium chloride.

Reading about God, whom many of us know as a God of grace and mercy, punishing Uzzah and Lot's wife and Ananias and Sapphira so severely should make us uncomfortable. And it should make us think critically about the relationship between justice and mercy. But even if we struggle to come to terms with God's actions in these Scriptures, these stories can teach us important truths about God's hopes and expectations for us.

QUESTIONS

1. In your opinion, did Uzzah (the steward of the ark of the covenant who touched the ark to keep it from tumbling from the cart on which it was being carried) deserve to lose his life as a consequence of touching the ark?

2. Imagine that someone with no previous knowledge of Scripture read about God's punishment of Uzzah in 1 Samuel 6 or of Lot's wife in Genesis 19. What impression of God might that person take from these Scriptures? How might you help that person better know and understand God?

3. Verse 8 tells us that David "got angry because of the LORD's anger lashed out against Uzzah." How did David know the reason for Uzzah's death?

4. According to verse 9, "David was frightened by the LORD that day." What place does the fear of God have in the life of a believer today? How does our connection with Jesus affect the way we approach God?

5. Christians profess a God of grace who is "compassionate and merciful, very patient, and full of faithful love" (Psalm 103:8) and who sent a Son into the world "that the world might be saved through him" (John 3:17). How do we reconcile this understanding of God with the picture of God we see in the stories of Uzzah and Ananias and Sapphira?

6. According to the Common English Bible translation, the Lord struck Uzzah because of his "mistake." Other translations use similar words, such as "error"; and at least one uses "irreverence," for the Hebrew word *shal*. In light of this, do you believe that God overreacted by striking Uzzah? Why, or why not?

7. John Wesley, the eighteenth-century founder of the Methodist movement, wrote that human beings are "improper judges of the actions of God" and "God's judgments are always just." Do you agree or disagree? Explain your answer.

8. Was God making an example of Uzzah for the benefit of others? How might that have been considered an act of mercy toward all of the people God didn't strike down for their sins?

2

GOD AND VIOLENCE
ARE WE ROOTING FOR THE RIGHT TEAM?

SCRIPTURE
1 KINGS 18:20-40

²⁰Ahab sent the message to all the Israelites. He gathered the prophets at Mount Carmel. ²¹Elijah approached all the people and said, "How long will you hobble back and forth between two opinions? If the LORD is God, follow God. If Baal is God, follow Baal." The people gave no answer.

²²Elijah said to the people, "I am the last of the LORD's prophets, but Baal's prophets number four hundred fifty. ²³Give us two bulls. Let Baal's prophets choose one. Let them cut it apart and set it on the wood, but don't add fire. I'll prepare the other bull, put it on the wood, but won't add fire. ²⁴Then all of you will call on the name of your god, and I will call on the name of the LORD. The god who answers with fire—that's the real God!"

All the people answered, "That's an excellent idea."

²⁵So Elijah said to the prophets of Baal, "Choose one of these bulls. Prepare it first since there are so many of you. Call on the name of your god, but don't add fire."

²⁶So they took one of the bulls that had been brought to them. They prepared it and called on Baal's name from morning to midday. They said, "Great Baal, answer us!" But there was no sound or answer. They performed a hopping dance around the altar that had been set up.

²⁷Around noon, Elijah started making fun of them: "Shout louder! Certainly he's a god! Perhaps he is lost in thought or wandering or traveling somewhere. Or maybe he is asleep and must wake up!"

²⁸So the prophets of Baal cried with a louder voice and cut themselves with swords and knives as was their custom. Their blood flowed all over them. ²⁹As noon passed they went crazy with their ritual until it was time for the evening offering. Still there was no sound or answer, no response whatsoever.

³⁰Then Elijah said to all the people, "Come here!" All the people closed in, and he repaired the Lord's altar that had been damaged. ³¹Elijah took twelve stones, according to the number of the tribes of the sons of Jacob—to whom the Lord's word came: "Your name will be Israel." ³²He built the stones into an altar in the Lord's name, and he dug a trench around the altar big enough to hold two seahs of dry grain. ³³He put the wood in order, butchered the bull, and placed the bull on the wood.

"Fill four jars with water and pour it on the sacrifice and on the wood," he commanded. ³⁴"Do it a second time!" he said. So they did it a second time. "Do it a third time!" And so they did it a third time. ³⁵The water flowed around the altar, and even the trench filled with water. ³⁶At the time of the evening offering, the prophet Elijah drew near and prayed: "Lᴏʀᴅ, the God of Abraham, Isaac, and Israel, let it be known today that you are God in Israel and that I am your servant. I have done all these things at your instructions. ³⁷Answer me, Lᴏʀᴅ! Answer me so that this people will know that you, Lᴏʀᴅ, are the real God and that you can change their hearts." ³⁸Then the Lᴏʀᴅ's fire fell; it consumed the sacrifice, the wood, the stones, and the dust. It even licked up the water in the trench!

³⁹All the people saw this and fell on their faces. "The Lᴏʀᴅ is the real God! The Lᴏʀᴅ is the real God!" they exclaimed.

⁴⁰Elijah said to them, "Seize Baal's prophets! Don't let any escape!" The people seized the prophets, and Elijah brought them to the Kishon Brook and killed them there.

INSIGHT AND IDEAS

During the 2012 National Hockey League playoffs, my Nashville Predators were considered contenders for the Stanley Cup. The Preds posted the third best record in a tough Western Conference and boasted arguably the best tandem of defensemen in the league in Shea Weber and Ryan Suter. (Suter left for Minnesota that summer. But this lesson isn't about forgiveness, so I won't go into that.)

Nashville faced the Detroit Red Wings, one of hockey's great franchises, in the first round of the playoffs. The Red Wings, one of the NHL's "Original Six" teams, had won eleven Stanley Cups. My Predators, founded in 1997, had only once advanced into the second round of the playoffs. Nashville fans consider the Red Wings our greatest rival, even if Detroit fans don't feel the same way about the Preds.

During the closing moments of Game 1, Detroit center Henrik Zetterberg hit Weber. Weber responded by slamming Zetterberg's head into the glass. Zetterberg's initial hit was common by hockey standards. But Weber's retaliation was well beyond the bounds of what is acceptable. It was reckless and dangerous. The league fined Weber $2,500 (the maximum permitted under the league's collective bargaining agreement) but did not suspend him. The Predators won that game 3-2.

Although I am a Predators fan, I wanted the league to suspend Weber. Zetterberg skated away from the incident unscathed, but Weber's behavior was malicious and could have caused serious injury. The NHL has suspended other players for far less egregious actions. The sports media outside of Nashville was nearly unanimous in its view that Weber deserved a suspension. And when the suspension didn't come through, I worried that my team had been given an unfair advantage and that I was rooting for the bad guys.

The Preds ended up losing Game 2 (the game that Weber would have missed had he been suspended) then won Games 3, 4, and 5 to take the series 4-1. So everything worked out. But on that one night when Shea Weber took the ice in his mustard yellow Predators sweater despite having assaulted Henrik Zetterberg two days earlier, I felt like I was on the wrong side. My Nashville Predators, the young upstarts who were poised to unseat the mighty Detroit Red Wings, had become the villains.

FROM UNDERDOG TO AGGRESSOR

In the previous session, I mentioned that the story of David dancing for joy as the ark of the covenant arrives in Jerusalem comes up frequently in youth ministry curriculum. The youth ministry canon also includes a pair of Scriptures involving the prophet Elijah and his relationship to King Ahab, Queen Jezebel, and the prophets of the Canaanite god Baal.

The first is the battle of the bonfires (1 Kings 18:20-39). Ahab, king of Israel, was fed up with Elijah and called him "the one who troubles Israel" (1 Kings 18:17). Ahab had set up a shrine to the Canaanite god Baal. And to send a message to Ahab and Israel, God had sent a three-year drought. Elijah, the troublemaker, had had the unfortunate assignment of telling Ahab that the drought was on its way (1 Kings 17:1). So to Ahab, Elijah was the "Drought Guy."

Since the drought didn't inspire any change in Ahab's regime, Elijah the Drought Guy posed a challenge to Ahab and the prophets of the Canaanite gods Baal and Asherah.

Hundreds of prophets gathered on Mount Carmel to accept Elijah's challenge. The terms of the challenge were simple: Each side (the God side and the Baal side) would choose a bull to prepare as a sacrifice. They would prepare their bulls and place them on an altar; but they would not start the fire. Their respective gods would be responsible for providing the fire.

The prophets of Baal prepared their bull, placed it on the altar, called on their god to bring fire, and performed a "hopping dance" (verse 26) to get Baal's attention. Nothing happened, so Elijah got snarky. "Perhaps he is lost in thought or wandering or traveling somewhere," Elijah said. Baal's prophets yelled louder and even cut themselves. Still, nothing happened.

When it was Elijah's turn, he raised the degree of difficulty by dousing the altar in water. Then he called on God, and God brought a fire that consumed everything, including the water. Elijah won. He had demonstrated that the God of Israel was for real and that Baal was powerless.

In the second Elijah Scripture in the youth ministry canon, Elijah is on the run for his life. King Ahab and Queen Jezebel were out to kill Elijah, and the prophet sought refuge in the wilderness. God provided for Elijah and eventually met him on Mount Horeb (the mountain on which God gave the law to Moses): "A very strong wind tore through the mountains and broke apart the stones before the Lord. But the Lord wasn't in the wind. After the wind, there was an earthquake. But the Lord wasn't in the earthquake. After the earthquake, there was a fire. But the Lᴏʀᴅ wasn't in the fire. After the fire, there was a sound. Thin. Quiet" (1 Kings 19:11-12). God then spoke to Elijah in the stillness and silence.

When we read this story through verse 39 then skip ahead to chapter 19, we have a narrative about an underdog named Elijah with a flair for the dramatic who proves that his God is living and active and that Baal, his opponents' god, is an idol that can't stand up to scrutiny but who ends up as a fugitive in the desert, where God cares for him.

But when we read to verse 40, the story changes. Elijah wasn't on the run because he showed up the prophets of Baal. He was on the run because he killed them. After the people gathered for the battle of bonfires realized that the God of Israel, and not Baal, was the One True God, Elijah had the people round up Baal's prophets so that he could kill them. And with that, the underdog became the aggressor.

Granted, Queen Jezebel, who was from Phoenicia and had supported Baal worship in Israel, had "killed the Lᴏʀᴅ's prophets" (1 Kings 18:4). So Elijah just responded in turn. But do we want a hero who behaves no differently than the villain? Can we root for a prophet who slaughters his rivals?

AND THE WALLS CAME TUMBLING DOWN

God and God's people are responsible for quite a few mass killings in Scripture. Some of these happen in the context of war, for the purpose of protecting God's people from ruthless and powerful foreign empires. For instance, Assyria was on the verge of conquering the southern kingdom of Judah (much as Assyria had already conquered the northern kingdom of Israel) before God wiped out 185,000 Assyrian soldiers, forcing prince and military leader Sennacherib to retreat (2 Kings 19:35-36). (Assyrian sources put a different spin on the story.) Lord Byron's poem "The Destruction of Sennacherib" recalls this event in anapestic tetrameter.

Other cases of divine slaughter in the Bible are more difficult to understand or justify.

I am named for an ancient Israelite hero: Joshua. He "fit the battle of Jericho," in the words of a popular African-American spiritual. And, of course, the walls came tumbling down.

I learned the story of Joshua and the battle of Jericho at a young age. I even had one of those book and audiocassette sets, so popular among children in the 1980s, that told the story of Joshua's victory. (The cassette told the story, and the listener followed along in the book.) When I was a child, the battle of Jericho was my favorite story in all of Scripture.

Jericho is a city in the current-day West Bank whose history dates back almost all the way to the beginning of human civilization. When Joshua led the Israelites into the Promised Land of Canaan after Moses' death, Jericho was the first major city they encountered. He sent a pair of spies ahead of the group to scout out the land, Jericho in particular. All we know of the spies' work is, "They set out and entered the house of a prostitute named Rahab" (Joshua 2:1). So it looks like, as soon as they got their scouting assignment, they headed for the brothel. Even so, the king of Jericho learned that Israelite spies were in his city and demanded that the prostitute Rahab hand them over. Rahab successfully hid the spies after reaching an agreement with them that she and her family would be spared when Israel sacked the city.

Scripture tells us that Joshua and the Israelites brought down Jericho's walls, not with traditional military tactics and technology but by marching around the city, blowing trumpets, and shouting. When the walls fell, the Israelites attacked. "Without mercy, they wiped out everything in the city as something reserved for God—man and woman, young and old, cattle, sheep, and donkeys" (Joshua 6:21).

What did the people (and animals) of Jericho do to deserve this treatment? As a child, I assumed that the people of Jericho were wicked. But the Bible says no such thing. Scripture suggests that Jericho's only crime was being in the way. God had promised Israel the land of Canaan, which had been the home of their ancestors. When Joshua and the Israelites moved into Canaan, they had to do something about the people who were already there. Starting with Jericho, Israel tore through the Promised Land, indiscriminately killing Canaanite men, women, and children. In *God Behaving Badly,* David T. Lamb argues that the guilt of the Canaanites and the right of Abraham's ancestors to the land of Canaan had been established in the Book of Genesis.[1] But can we root for a people who

---

1 From *God Behaving Badly*; pages 40–43.

punishes entire cities for something that had happened hundreds of years earlier?

How is it that God, who elsewhere in the Old Testament commands God's people to love their neighbors and to treat the foreigners living among them as citizens (Leviticus 19:18, 34), blesses and participates in genocide? There is no easy solution to this problem. When we encounter texts in which God's people slaughter their neighbors and adversaries, it's important to ask what role God plays in the violence. Is God directly responsible (as in the destruction of Sennacherib's army)? Do God's people act with God's blessing and according to God's instruction (as in the battle of Jericho)? Or are the people acting on their own?

Depending on one's understanding of the authority and inspiration of Scripture, one might also look critically at the text itself. Are these ancient writings historical accounts of God's activities or are they the writer's interpretations of how God was at work in the story of God's people? Might the scribes who recorded accounts of these events have misunderstood God's role in Israel's violent conquests?

'MY CREATURES ARE DROWNING IN THE SEA'

If you've spent much time in children's and/or youth ministry, you've probably encountered the song "Pharaoh Pharaoh." The song—set to the tune of "Louie Louie," by Richard Berry and made famous by The Kingsmen—tells the story of the Exodus. It begins with the call of Moses and ends with the people of Israel escaping from Egypt through

36

the Red Sea, or Sea of Reeds. The waters part, allowing
the Israelites to pass through on dry land; but when the
pursuing Egyptians attempt to follow, the waters recede,
drowning the entire Egyptian army. The verse of the song
that describes Israel's victory at the Red Sea says that
Pharaoh's army "did the dead man's float."

Even as a child I had trouble singing that line. Yes, Pharaoh
and his army were the bad guys, the ones who had
enslaved the Israelites and refused to let them go. Still,
celebrating the demise of hundreds and possibly thousands
of Egyptian soldiers to the tune of one of the catchiest
three-chord pop songs in rock 'n' roll history never sat right
with me.

After the Israelites passed through the sea and escaped
from Egypt, they celebrated. Moses led the men in song,
and his sister, the prophet Miriam, led the women. Miriam's
song, as recorded in Exodus 15:21, was simple: "Sing to the
LORD for an overflowing victory! Horse and rider he threw
into the sea!"

In their book *The Meaning of the Bible,* scholars Douglas A.
Knight and Amy-Jill Levine mention a well known *midrash*
that elaborates on the celebration in Exodus 15. *Midrash*
are interpretive studies of passages in the *Tanakh* (the
Jewish Bible, which is similar in content to the Christian Old
Testament) by Jewish rabbis. This particular midrash, from
the Babylonian Talmud, says that the angels in heaven joined
in the celebration of the Egyptians' defeat and sang along
with Moses, Miriam, and the rest of the people of Israel. But

God did not: "Searching, the angels found God weeping. When they inquired, God responded, 'My creatures are drowning in the sea and you want to sing praises?'"[2]

There is no midrash in Christian tradition. But perhaps we can benefit from the wisdom of this rabbi and others who have wrestled with the question of God's role in the destruction of the Egyptians, Canaanites, prophets of Baal, and Assyrians. Perhaps there is a place for love and grace amid the violence.

2 From *The Meaning of the Bible,* by Douglas A. Knight and Amy-Jill Levine (HarperOne, 2011); page 139, citing the Babylonian Talmud *Megilla* 10b.

QUESTIONS

1. In your opinion, was Elijah's slaughter of the prophets of Baal justified? Why, or why not?

2. What would have been the alternative to killing the prophets of Baal? How might this alternative reality have played out? What information could be missing in this account that would help us understand Elijah's actions in this difficult passage?

3. If possible divide into pairs or small groups. Have each group look at one of the following Scriptures: Exodus 11:1-10; 12:29-30 (the plague of the firstborn); Exodus 14:5-31 (the parting of the sea); Joshua 5:13-6:27 (the battle of Jericho); 2 Kings 19:20-37 (the fall of Sennacherib's army). If your numbers don't allow you to divide into small groups, have individuals look up each text. Have each group or person consider the following questions:

What role does God play in the violence and killing?

How, if at all, is the violence and killing justified?

What problems does this Scripture pose?

What does this Scripture teach us about God and God's people?

4. Christians profess a God of grace who is "compassionate and merciful, very patient, and full of faithful love" (Psalm 103:8) and who sent a Son into the world "that the world might be saved through him" (John 3:17). How do we reconcile this understanding of God with Scriptures that show God blessing or participating in violence on a large scale?

5. What questions or concerns do you have about God's role in these mass killings? Where or to whom might you go for wisdom and answers?

6. How might the midrash about the Israelites' celebration of their defeat of Egypt help us when we struggle with God's role in violent and difficult Scriptures?

3

HARD SAYINGS
HATRED AND DISMEMBERMENT—FOR JESUS?

SCRIPTURE
MATTHEW 5:27-30; LUKE 14:25-27

MATTHEW 5:27-30

27"You have heard that it was said, *Don't commit adultery*. 28But I say to you that every man who looks at a woman lustfully has already committed adultery in his heart. 29And if your right eye causes you to fall into sin, tear it out and throw it away. It's better that you lose a part of your body than that your whole body be thrown into hell. 30And if your right hand causes you to fall into sin, chop it off and throw it away. It's better that you lose a part of your body than that your whole body go into hell."

LUKE 14:25-27

25Large crowds were traveling with Jesus. Turning to them, he said, 26"Whoever comes to me and doesn't hate father and mother, spouse and children, and brothers and sisters—yes, even one's own life—cannot be my disciple. [27]Whoever doesn't carry their own cross and follow me cannot be my disciple."

INSIGHT AND IDEAS

Do you have two hands and two eyes? Maybe you shouldn't.

Origen of Alexandria was one of the most prolific scholars and writers in church history and one of the church's first theologians. He was also a heretic.

Origen believed in the preexistence of souls and that a person's fortunes in this life were related to the actions of their souls in a previous state. He believed that these souls took the form of angels, demons, and human beings but that all souls would eventually be reconciled to God. Origen also held that Jesus Christ was subordinate to God the Father. The Second Council of Constantinople, in A.D. 553, formally anathematized Origen; and the church destroyed many of his writings in response to this condemnation.

Even though Origen's teachings were later deemed heretical, orthodox Christians can still learn from his lifestyle. Eusebius, the great historian of the early church, tells us that Origen put "away from him all inducements to youthful lusts, and at all times of the day disciplining himself by performing strenuous tasks, while he devoted most of the night to the study of Holy Scriptures. . . . He displayed an enthusiasm beyond his years, and patiently enduring cold and nakedness went to the furthest limit of poverty. . . . [It] is said that for several years he went about on foot without any shoes at all, and for a much longer period abstained from wine and all else beyond the minimum of food."[1]

But Origen's asceticism went beyond fasting and eschewing worldly goods. Eusebius also tells us that this great theologian of the early church also castrated himself. Origen apparently decided to become a eunuch in accordance with Jesus' teaching in Matthew 19:12: "There are eunuchs who have been eunuchs from birth. And there are eunuchs who have been made eunuchs by other people. And there are eunuchs who have made themselves eunuchs because of the kingdom of heaven. Those who can accept it should accept it."

Jesus doesn't command anyone to castrate himself; he just says that some have chosen to do so "because of the kingdom of heaven." But Jesus does teach dismemberment elsewhere in Matthew's Gospel.

In his Sermon on the Mount, Jesus commanded his followers to adhere to a higher standard than that which is proscribed by the Jewish Law. He said that it's not enough to avoid murder; we must also avoid rage. It's not enough to avoid false pledges; we must avoid all sorts of pledges and let our "*yes* mean yes" and our "*no* mean no" (Matthew 5:37). It's not enough to love our neighbor; we must also love our enemies.

---

1 From *The History of the Church From Christ to Constantine*, by Eusebius, translated by G.A. Williamson (Augsburg, 1965); pages 243–244.

Regarding adultery, Jesus taught that, in addition to not having sex with another person's spouse, we should also avoid looking at women "lustfully" (Matthew 5:28). (Jesus said nothing about looking at men lustfully, but I'm guessing that the same principle applies.) He then goes a step further and says that, if our right eye causes us to sin (such as by looking at someone lustfully), we should "tear it out and throw it away" (Matthew 5:29). Likewise, he says, if our right hand causes us to sin, we should "chop it off and throw it away" (5:30).

Does Jesus really want us to respond to sin and temptation by removing body parts?

THE TRUMP CARD

Jesus is our trump card. As Christians, we profess that Jesus is God in human form and that we know God most fully through Jesus. When we're faced with an uncomfortable text from elsewhere in Scripture, we can pull Jesus from our hand and make everything better. We don't worry about the accounts of God's people completely annihilating their enemies, because Jesus tells us to "love [our] enemies and pray for those who harass [us]" (Matthew 5:44). We don't worry about accounts of God smiting people for seemingly minor offenses, because we have accounts of Jesus forgiving those who denied and tortured him.

But, if you read through all of what Jesus teaches in the four biblical Gospels, you'll discover that not all of his teachings are as palatable as "treat people in the same way that you want people to treat you" (Matthew 7:12) or the parable of the mustard seed (Mark 4:30-32).

We've already seen that, in his Sermon on the Mount, Jesus taught that we should tear out eyeballs and chop off hands to avoid sin. Jesus also compared a Canaanite woman to a dog (Matthew 15:21-28), suggested that it's impossible for a rich person to "enter God's kingdom" (Luke 18:25), and taught that his followers should hate their "father and mother, spouse and children."

Yes, Jesus—the Jesus who teaches us to love our neighbors (even those who happen to belong to a rival ethnic or religious group) and our enemies—tells us to hate those who are closest to us. He says, "Whoever comes to me and doesn't hate father and mother, spouse and children, and brothers and sisters—yes, even one's own life—cannot be my disciple" (Luke 14:26). Hating spouses and children doesn't seem consistent with the love that pervades the rest of Jesus' teaching. When asked which commandment was greatest, Jesus responded with two, both of which involved love: First, love God. Second, "Love your neighbor as you love yourself" (Matthew 22:39, citing Leviticus 19:18). On the final evening before his death, Jesus told his disciples, "This is my commandment: love each other just as I have loved you" (John 15:12).

So how can we hate our friends and family and remain true to the rest of Jesus' instructions? Is *hate* really the word Jesus was going for here? Could there be a translation error?

There's certainly no error in translation. The original Greek doesn't give us much wiggle room. The word Jesus uses that we translate as "hate" is *miseo*. And while there are plenty of Greek words that don't have a direct English equivalent, *miseo* is not

45

one of those words. It means "hate." And when *miseo* appears elsewhere in the New Testament, it's obvious that "hate" is the intended meaning (for example, 1 John 3:15, which says, "Everyone who hates a brother or sister is a murderer").

HATERS GONNA HATE

The term *player hater* emerged from 1990's hip-hop culture. The late Notorious B.I.G. was especially fond of the term. The word *player* had come to represent anyone who was especially successful. The term often took on sexual connotations but could also refer to someone who was successful in sports or business. A player hater was anyone who, usually out of jealousy, dismisses or belittles a player's accomplishments.

Because language often evolves by abbreviation and because the "hate" once reserved for players is now available to anyone with the audacity to create something or state an opinion, "player" disappeared over time, leaving us with "hater."

To hate means to despise or passionately dislike. And in most cases, a hater's "hate" doesn't rise to that level of disdain. The average hater who refuses to recognize LeBron James as one of the greatest players in basketball history (either out of lingering displeasure about the way James handled free agency in 2010 or as a backlash against media personalities who have taken to comparing James to Michael Jordan) doesn't actually hate LeBron James. And the average hater who insists that *The Avengers* wasn't nearly as good as critics and fanboys made it out to be doesn't truly hate Joss Whedon or Marvel Comics or even the film itself. Yet we use the word *hate*. Yes, the same word we use to describe words and actions meant to denigrate and intimidate entire populations is the word we use to describe uncharitable Internet banter. Obviously, there are situations where "hate" isn't actually hate.

LITERALLY OR FIGURATIVELY?

R. Alan Culpepper says in *The New Interpreter's Bible* commentary on Luke 14:26 that Jesus' demand that his followers hate their closest family members is "a Semitic hyperbole that exaggerates a contrast so that it can be seen more clearly. . . . It indicates that if there is a conflict, one's response to the demands of discipleship must take precedence over even the most sacred of human relationships."[2] In other words, "hate" isn't actually hate.

Literacy requires us not only to translate letters and symbols into words and words into ideas but also to recognize devices such as exaggeration, figure of speech, metaphor, and sarcasm. These devices can be difficult to detect when we encounter them in our own language and culture. (Consider, for example, the Tumblr site Literally Unbelievable,[3] which compiles Facebook posts by those who

---

2 From "Luke 14:25-35, Conditions for Discipleship," by R. Alan Culpepper, in *The New Interpreter's Bible*, Vol. 9 (Abingdon Press, 1995); page 290.
3 From *http://www.literallyunbelievable.org*.

fail to see the satire in articles from the satirical website and newspaper *The Onion*.) How much more difficult must it be to identify hyperbole and figure of speech in Jesus' teachings? Consider that Jesus spoke Aramaic and his words were recorded in Greek (possibly decades after his death and resurrection) then translated into English hundreds of years later.

Jesus tells us, in plain, clear words, to tear out our eye and chop off our hand. Considering that, aside from Origen, we have no examples from history of Jesus' followers removing their eyes and hands, it's quite possible that Jesus did not mean to be literal. Perhaps he was using the image of slicing off a hand or gouging out an eye to emphasize our need to eliminate—to "tear out" or "chop off"—anything in our life that tempts us to stray from God or violate Jesus' teachings. Those who struggle with gluttony, for instance (myself included), may need to remove all-you-can-eat restaurants from their life. Those who struggle with materialism may need to "chop off" (cut up) their credit cards.

This is not to say that we should rethink every teaching of Jesus that challenges us or makes us uncomfortable. Much of what Jesus said should make us uneasy. But don't tell your mother that you despise her, rip your eyeball out of its socket, or do what Origen did just because Jesus told you to. First, remember the complexities of language and translation and consider how Jesus might be using exaggeration or metaphor to get his point across.

QUESTIONS

1. When have you encountered a teaching or saying of Jesus that you weren't comfortable with? How did you respond? What questions do you still have about these teachings?

2. How can we in the twenty-first century, reading words written in another language two thousand years ago, determine when Jesus and biblical authors are speaking or writing literally and when they are using hyperbole, metaphor, or figure of speech?

3. What truths do we know about Jesus that help us better understand his teachings?

4. Is looking at someone lustfully the same on every level as actually committing adultery? How might a misunderstanding of Jesus' words here cause problems when this Scripture is applied to your life?

5. What point, do you think, is Jesus trying to make when he tells us to tear out an eye or chop off a hand if that body part causes us to sin? How does this teaching apply to your life?

6. How do Jesus' words in these passages challenge the conventional wisdom that Jesus is a contrast to the "harshness" of the Old Testament and presents a picture of a "kinder, gentler" God?

7. What, do you think, is Jesus telling us when he says that we should "hate father and mother, spouse and children, and brothers and sisters" and our own lives in order to be his disciples? How does this teaching apply to your life?

8. What is the connection Jesus is making in Matthew 5:29-30 between sin and hell?

9. Read the story of Jesus and the Canaanite woman (Matthew 15:21-28). Here the Greek for *dog* refers to a puppy or a house dog. Why would Jesus use that term to refer to a woman who had faith in him and desperately wanted him to heal her daughter? Could he have been using sarcasm or figurative speech? What do you think he meant?

10. In what ways are other Scripture passages helpful when we encounter tough passages from the Bible? What are some other tools we can use to help us make sense of the passages that are difficult to accept?

4

INCONSISTENT GOD?
GOBS OF GLORIOUS GRACE

SCRIPTURE
PSALM 103:1-14

¹Let my whole being bless the Lord!

Let everything inside me bless his holy name!

²Let my whole being bless the Lord

and never forget all his good deeds:

³how God forgives all your sins,

heals all your sickness,

⁴saves your life from the pit,

crowns you with faithful love and compassion,

⁵and satisfies you with plenty of good things

so that your youth is made fresh like an eagle's.

⁶The Lord works righteousness;

does justice for all who are oppressed.

⁷God made his ways known to Moses;

 made his deeds known to the Israelites.

⁸The Lᴏʀᴅ is compassionate and merciful,

 very patient, and full of faithful love.

⁹God won't always play the judge;

 he won't be angry forever.

¹⁰He doesn't deal with us according to our sin

 or repay us according to our wrongdoing,

  ¹¹because as high as heaven is above the earth,

 that's how large God's faithful love is for those who honor him.

¹²As far as east is from west—

 that's how far God has removed our sin from us.

¹³Like a parent feels compassion for their children—

 that's how the Lᴏʀᴅ feels compassion for those who honor him.

¹⁴Because God knows how we're made,

 God remembers we're just dust.

INSIGHT AND IDEAS

My younger son spent the better part of a school year singing in our congregation's "Cherub Choir" before mustering the courage to sing a single note in front of the congregation. During some of the choir's performances, he took his place on the chancel steps and froze, not moving his mouth or any other part of his body for the duration of the song. Other times, he refused to even walk to the front of the congregation with the rest of the choir.

But for the Cherub Choir's final performance of the year, my then three-year-old son stood with the rest of the group and sang a song called "Straight From the Heart of God." He sang every word. I don't remember every word, and I'm guessing that he doesn't either. But I'll never forget the first line: "Oh, I've got gobs and gobs of glorious grace, glorious grace, glorious grace."

These gobs of glorious grace about which my preschooler sang are what set Christianity apart from other faith traditions and worldviews. Christians believe that we do not, and cannot, earn salvation or fulfillment. It is a gift. We confess that God became human in the person of Jesus, suffered and died, and rose again to defeat death, make atonement for our sins, and allow us to live forever in God's eternal kingdom. We believe, on one hand, that all people and all of creation are broken but, on the other hand, that God is working constantly to redeem creation and will one day make all things new.

We encounter this grace throughout Scripture. Psalm 103, for example, praises God's mercy and compassion and patience, the magnitude of God's love, and God's willingness to forgive. In Romans 3:23-24, the apostle Paul says, "All have sinned and fall short of God's glory, but all are treated as righteous freely by his grace because of a ransom that was paid by Christ Jesus."

But as we have seen, there are plenty of events and teachings recorded in the Bible in which grace appears to be absent. Where was the grace in God's punishment of

Uzzah or in the destruction of Jericho? One of the most difficult stories in all of Scripture, in my opinion, involves God's rejection of King Saul. God had told Saul, "Attack the Amalekites; put everything that belongs to them under the ban. Spare no one. Kill men and women, children and infants, oxen and sheep, camels and donkeys" (1 Samuel 15:3). Saul led Israel to a decisive victory over Amalek, but he neglected to kill Agag, the Amalekite king. He also spared some sheep and cattle. Because Saul failed to destroy every single living being in Amalek, God regretted the decision to make Saul king and sent the prophet Samuel to anoint David as Saul's successor. Where's the grace?

THE MARCION CHRONICLES

Try this. Google "Old Testament God New Testament God." Barring a sea change in Internet theology between the time I am writing this and the time you humor me by typing those six words into the Google search bar, you will find dozens (and probably hundreds) of links to articles and question-and-answer threads dedicated to reconciling the hot-tempered and capricious God of the Old Testament with the loving and gracious father of the New Testament.

Pitting the Old Testament God against the New Testament God is a common technique used to explain away Old Testament texts that seem to be lacking in grace. Sure, the idea goes, God used to be angry and temperamental, but then Jesus came along, voided all the old nasty stuff, and replaced it with grace.

The idea that the character and demeanor of God in the Old Testament is inconsistent with that of God in the New Testament goes back to a second-century bishop named Marcion of Sinope. (I've heard different pronunciations of Marcion's name, but my church history professor in divinity school pronounced it "Martian." So that's how I say it.) Marcion concluded that the God of the Old Testament and the God of Jesus Christ were wholly incompatible and that God's old covenant with Israel could not be reconciled with God's new covenant through Christ. Marcion eschewed all of the Old Testament writings and removed all references to Judaism from the Gospel of Luke, the one Gospel he considered authoritative. Marcion's Bible consisted only of his version of Luke and ten of Paul's letters.

Marcion's teachings earned him an excommunication and a place on the list of history's most notorious heretics. But the idea that the God of the Old Testament and the God of the New are incompatible obviously didn't disappear when Marcion was expelled. It has stubbornly persisted for centuries and even pops up in the 1984 film *Ghostbusters*, the second greatest movie ever made. (*Back to the Future* is first.) When Dr. Peter Venkman (Bill Murray) warns the mayor of New York that "the city is headed for a disaster of biblical proportions," Dr. Ray Stantz (Dan Akroyd) clarifies: "What he means is Old Testament, Mr. Mayor, real wrath of God type stuff."

Knight and Levine in *The Meaning of the Bible* say that such a distinction between "the Old Testament God of wrath" and "the New Testament God of love" both "misreads the theology of both Testaments" and "results in anti-Jewish propaganda and misguided Christian apologetic."[1]

Grace is by no means absent in the Old Testament. In the Bible's opening pages in the Book of Genesis we see God respond with grace to Cain's murder of his brother Abel. God holds Cain accountable for his crime, sentencing him to the life of a "roving nomad" (Genesis 4:12). But God does not take Cain's life. Instead God "put a sign on Cain so that no one who found him would assault him" (4:15). Likewise, God's wrath does not disappear when the page numbers in our Bibles reset to "1." We've already looked at the death of Ananias and Sapphira. And Jesus, for his part, uses the phrase "weeping and gnashing of teeth" six times in Matthew alone (Matthew 8:12; 13:42; 13:50; 22:13; 24:51; 25:30, NRSV). In two of these cases the weeping and teeth gnashing happens in the "outer darkness"; in two others it happens in a "furnace of fire."

According to historical, orthodox Christianity, and according to the Bible itself, there is no inconsistency between the Old Testament God of Israel and the New Testament God of Jesus. God's mercy and God's justice (and wrath) are at work throughout Scripture, in both the Old and New Testaments.

---

1 From *The Meaning of the Bible*; pages 137–138.

WATERS OF GRACE, AND DEATH

Water is a big deal for Christians. (It's a big deal for humans in general, since water accounts for about 60 percent of our body weight,[2] but it's especially important for Christians.) Most Christians recognize the ritual of baptism as a sacrament—a rite ordained by Jesus himself in which God's grace is at work in a unique way. And baptism involves water.

The waters of baptism—whether they are applied by sprinkling, pouring, or immersion—are cleansing. They wash away our sin. During the sacrament of baptism we recall the waters of the Jordan River with which John the Baptist baptized Jesus and the waters from rivers, lakes, oceans, and baptismal fonts around the world that have initiated young children and new converts into the faith over the past two millennia. But the role of water in cleansing and redemption predates the beginning of Jesus' earthly ministry and the emergence of Christianity. It goes all the way back to creation.

The baptismal liturgy in my tradition, United Methodism, recalls the role of water in God's ongoing work of creation and redemption. It starts at the beginning, when God "swept across the dark waters and brought forth light." It then fast forwards to the time of Noah, when God "saved those on the ark through water," then to the Exodus and God leading the people of Israel "to freedom through the sea."

---

2 From *http://www.mayoclinic.com/health/water/NU00283*. Accessed 20 Nov. 2013.

This liturgy describes the water in these episodes as an agent of grace. The water delivers God's people first from annihilation and then from oppression. But these waters are as deadly and destructive as they are redemptive. The waters that "saved those on the ark" wiped out the remainder of the human species. Where we see grace in this baptismal liturgy we also see judgment and violence. On the other hand, where we see judgment and violence, we also see grace.

GLIMPSES OF GRACE

When God punished Cain for the murder of his brother Abel by forcing him to live as a nomad, God also put a mark on Cain to ensure that no one would harm him. When Abraham pleaded with God not to destroy the innocent and righteous people of Sodom, God gave Abraham multiple opportunities to locate such people. (Abraham was unsuccessful.) One of the most perplexing Scriptures for the ancient rabbis was the binding of Isaac in Genesis 22, in which God commands Abraham to sacrifice his son Isaac. While people of faith continue to be troubled by God's deciding to test Abraham's faith by commanding him to sacrifice his child—and while biblical readers are left to wonder what Sarah was doing and thinking while this was going down—grace is not absent in this narrative. Instead of allowing Abraham to take Isaac's life, God provides an alternative sacrifice.

After Jesus refers to a Canaanite woman as a dog (Matthew 15:22-28), possibly sarcastically, he praises her faith and heals her daughter. And after Jesus tells a wealthy man to give up all of his possessions and says that a rich man is less likely to enter God's kingdom than a camel is to walk through the eye of a needle, Jesus says that what is impossible for human beings is possible for God (Matthew 19:16-26).

Even when grace seems to be missing from a particular text, we can sometimes find it by looking at the entirety of Scripture. The prophet Ezra tore his "clothes and cloak" and "pulled out hair" from his head and beard when he learned that many of God's people had married foreign wives. In the Book of Ezra, a council of leaders in Judah resolved this matter by deporting all foreign women who had married men of Judah. But lest we think that the Bible teaches miscegenation and tearing apart families, the Book of Ruth, which many scholars believe was written around the same time as Ezra, offers a different perspective. The hero and title character is a woman from Moab who moves to Israel with her mother-in-law, marries an Israelite man, and becomes the great-grandmother of David, Israel's greatest king.

The entire Book of Nahum is an oracle about the destruction of the Assyrian city of Nineveh. Nahum says about Nineveh, "Look! I am against you, proclaims the Lord of heavenly forces. I will lift your skirts over your face; I will show nations your nakedness and kingdoms your dishonor. I will throw disgusting things at you; I will treat you with contempt and make you a spectacle" (Nahum 3:5-6). Harsh. But elsewhere in the minor prophets, we find Jonah, whom God sends to Nineveh to warn the people there of God's impending wrath. The people of Nineveh repent; and God, to Jonah's displeasure, relents. "Can't I pity Nineveh," God asks Jonah, "that great city, in which there are more than one hundred twenty thousand people who can't tell their right hand from their left, and also many animals?" (Jonah 4:11).

When we encounter texts that seem inconsistent with a God who protected Cain, blessed Ruth, and pitied the Ninevites, we need to consider the role that God plays in these Scriptures and the role that human beings play. God's people may do horrible things that God neither blesses nor facilitates. We must also discern the difference between what God is doing and what God's people perceive God to be doing.

Even so, there will be Scriptures that we continue to struggle with, Scriptures for which we struggle to find answers. We may seldom or never read these texts in worship or teach them to children and youth or reflect on them as part of our daily devotional time. But these uncomfortable texts are part of our canon, our collection of sacred and authoritative writings. So we can't dismiss them or pretend that they aren't there. We must embrace the struggle and always look for evidence of God's grace. If we do, we might find gobs of it.

QUESTIONS

1. Read Psalm 103:1-14. What do these verses tell us about God's grace? How do these verses inform our reading of difficult and perplexing texts?

2. Psalm 103:3 says that God "forgives all your sins" and "heals all your sickness." What does this mean? How does this verse apply to believers today?

3. Which Scriptures (whether texts that you've explored in this study or others) are most difficult for you to come to terms with? Where, if anywhere, do you see God's grace at play in these Scriptures?

4. Have you encountered the idea that the God of the Old Testament is different from or incompatible with the God of the New Testament? Why, do you think, is this idea so persistent? What are the flaws in this idea?

5. How can we reconcile God's justice and wrath with God's grace and mercy? How do grace and wrath contradict each other? How, if at all, do they complement each other?

6. What evidence do you see of God's grace, whether in Scripture or from your personal experience?

7. Psalm 103:9 tells us, "God won't always play the judge; he won't be angry forever." What insights can we draw from this verse about the complexity of God's personality? How do we reconcile this verse with the idea that God is unchanging?

8. How do your unanswered questions about God and the Bible affect your faith? How can you use such mysteries in a constructive way as you walk with Christ?

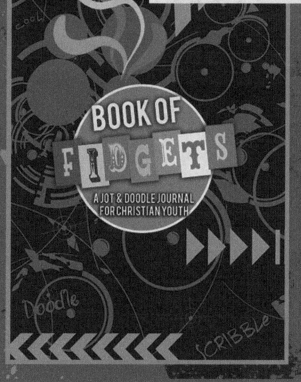

CONVERGE

Bible Studies

is the right topical short-term study series for you!

WOMEN OF THE BIBLE
by James A. Harnish
9781426771545

OUR COMMON SINS
by Dottie Escobedo-Frank
9781426768989

WHO YOU ARE IN CHRIST
by Shane Raynor
9781426771538

RECLAIMING ANGER
by David Dorn
9781426771552

SHARING THE GOSPEL
by Curtis Zackery
9781426771569

THREE GIFTS, ONE CHRIST
by Katie Z. Dawson
9781426778278

KINGDOM BUILDING
by Grace Biskie
9781426771576

WHO IS JESUS?
by Adam Thomas
9781426778292

PRACTICAL PRAYER
by Joseph Yoo
9781426778254

And more to come.

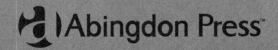

Abingdon Press™

BKM147020004 PACP01463307-01

CPSIA information can be obtained at www.ICGtesting.com
Printed in the USA
LVOW05s0729300115

424914LV00004B/8/P

9 781426 789533